WITHDRAWN

D1528549

CELEBRATING HOLIDAYS

Celebrating
Veterans
Day

Elaine Landau

Enslow Elementary

an imprint of

Enslow Publishers, Inc.

40 Industrial Road
Box 398
Berkeley Heights, NJ 07922
USA

http://www.enslow.com

To Jason Garmizo

Enslow Elementary, an imprint of Enslow Publishers, Inc.

Enslow Elementary® is a registered trademark of Enslow Publishers, Inc.

Original edition published as *Veterans Day: Remembering Our War Heroes* in 2002.

Library of Congress Cataloging-in-Publication Data

Landau, Elaine.
    Celebrating Veterans Day / Elaine Landau.
        p. cm.—(Celebrating holidays)
    Summary: "Read about our war heroes and how we celebrate and honor them with
    a special day"—Provided by publisher.
    Includes bibliographical references and index.
    ISBN 978-0-7660-4036-6 (alk. paper)
        1. Veterans Day—Juvenile literature. I. Title.
D671.L357 2012
394.264—dc23   2011021031

Future Editions
Paperback ISBN 978-1-59845-403-1
ePUB ISBN 978-1-4645-1087-8
PDF ISBN 978-1-4646-1087-5

Printed in China.

012012 Leo Paper Group, Heshan City, Guangdong, China

10 9 8 7 6 5 4 3 2 1

Photo Credits: AP Images/Dima Gavrysh, p. 41; AP Images/Josh Anderson, p. 36; AP Images/Mike
Vogt, p. 23; AP Images/Rgelio Solis, p. 37; Cheryl Wells/Enslow Publishers, Inc., p. 44; © Corel
Corporation, pp. 3, 5, 8, 10, 15, 16, 24, 28, 29, 39, 40, 45, 47; Department of Defense, pp. 6, 10, 12, 13, 20,
30, 36, 38; Enslow Publishers, Inc., p. 29; JustASC/Shutterstock.com, p. 30; Library of Congress, p. 14;
MISHELLA/Shutterstock.com, p. 20; © 2011 Photos.com, a division of Getty Images. All rights
reserved., pp. 11, 19, 21, 22, 27, 31, 32, 35; © Shutterstock.com, pp. 26, 33, 34; Steve Ghiringhelli, The
Mountaineer, p. 4; Stockstudios/Shutterstock.com, p. 25 United States Coast Guard, p. 18; United States
Marines, p. 9; White House, p. 17.

Cover Photo: AP Images/Michael Patrick.

CONTENTS

In the United States, Americans hold elections to pick their leaders. President Barack Obama was elected president in 2009.

CHAPTER 1

LAND OF THE FREE

The United States of America is not ruled by a king or queen. Instead, Americans have elections. Citizens cast votes to pick their leaders.

These leaders stand up for the people. They serve in government and carry out the people's wishes. This form of government is known as a democracy. In a democracy, people have certain rights and freedoms.

Americans enjoy many freedoms. Among these is religious freedom. Americans can pray at a church, a temple, or a mosque, or not pray at all. It is up to them.

THE AMERICAN FLAG

There are fifty stars on the American flag. Each star stands for a state in the United States. There are thirteen stripes on the flag. These stripes stand for the original colonies that made up the United States when it was first formed. The colors on the flag are also important. Red stands for bravery. White stands for purity. Blue stands for justice.

Members of the United States Army
are very proud of the American flag.
They honor our flag and our country
in a special ceremony. This ceremony
is called Presenting the Colors.

People in the United States can also live where they want. They can pick any job they are able to do. They can even own a business.

Americans are free to travel, too. They can go anywhere. They do not need the government's permission. People in the United States love their freedom. But they know that other people worked very hard for that freedom.

Brave men and women have fought for America's freedom. These people have been members of the United States Armed Forces. The armed forces are made up of the men and women in the Army, Navy, Marines, Air Force, and Coast Guard.

Members of the armed forces protect and defend our nation. These loyal men and women have often fought against America's enemies. They have protected us without thinking about the danger to themselves.

Veterans are members of the armed forces who have fought in a war.

America is very grateful for its soldiers. All are heroes. Some died fighting for their country. But they all fought to protect the rights and freedom of American citizens.

This is Arlington National Cemetery, a famous cemetery for soldiers.

Parades are a fun way to thank America's soldiers for keeping us safe.

We show our respect for our veterans on a special day known as Veterans Day. Veterans Day is celebrated each year on November 11.

On Veterans Day, America thanks its veterans. There are parades. People place flowers on soldiers' graves. Veterans Day is a day to remember and thank the people who have kept our nation free.

In World War I, proud members of the United States Army, like these men, fought for our country. They fought against Germany and other countries that were on Germany's side.

CHAPTER 2

A SPECIAL DAY

American people have always fought for the United States. But America has not always had Veterans Day as a way to say thank you. This holiday began after a war known as World War I.

World War I involved the world's greatest powers. On one side was a group called the Allies. The Allies were made up of the countries of the United States, Britain, France, Italy, Russia, and other nations. They fought against Germany and other countries that were on Germany's side.

The bugle song "Taps" is played to say goodbye to soldiers who have died in battle.

TAPS

"Taps" was written during the time of the American Civil War, and is still played today.

Taps

Fading light dims the sight,
And a star gems the sky,
gleaming bright.
From afar drawing nigh-
falls the night.

Day is done, gone the sun,
From the lake, from the
hills, from the sky.
All is well, safely rest,
God is nigh.

Then good night,
peaceful night,
'Til the light of the dawn
shineth bright,
God is near, do not
fear-Friend, good night.

Most of the fighting in World War I was done in Europe. This picture shows an important battle in France called the Battle of the Somme.

World War I was fought between the years 1914 and 1918. There were many reasons for this war. A number of nations had become enemies. Each wanted to be the most powerful. Some wanted more land. That meant taking land belonging to other countries. It also meant going to war to get the land.

Most of the fighting in World War I took place in Europe. It was a long and hard war. About 10 million soldiers from both sides were killed. At least 20 million soldiers were wounded.

The famous 369th arrive in New York City. When World War I was over, members of the 369th Colored Infantry celebrated.

In the end, the Allies won. Early on the morning of November 11, 1918, the countries fighting the war agreed to make peace. At 11:00 A.M. that day, the fighting stopped.

Soldiers on battlefields put down their guns. They no longer had to use their weapons. They cheered and blew whistles instead.

The good news spread around the world. People hugged one another and danced in the streets. Some businesses closed. The owners and workers wanted to celebrate the end of the war, too.

Americans were glad the war was over. But they did not forget those who had fought. These soldiers were remembered the next year. On November 11, 1919, President Woodrow Wilson declared the day Armistice Day. It was the anniversary of the end of World War I. It was a day to honor the war's veterans.

World War I veterans continue to be remembered each year on November 11. One of the special places where the veterans are honored each year is at Arlington National Cemetery. It is in Arlington, Virginia. The cemetery holds the graves of men and women who served in the U.S. Armed Forces.

The Tomb of the Unknowns is near the center of the cemetery. It faces the Potomac River and Washington, D.C. Washington, D.C. is our nation's capital.

A soldier who died in World War I was placed in the tomb on November 11, 1921. No one knows his name. His body could not be identified. He stands for all of the World War I soldiers who died. On the tomb are the words:

He rests in honored glory
An American soldier known but to God

Many people sent flowers that were placed at the tomb.

Americans now had a place to honor World War I veterans. But they wanted Armistice Day to be an official holiday. People wrote to their lawmakers to ask them to help.

In 1926, November 11 was officially named Armistice Day. Twelve years later, in 1938, our lawmakers made Armistice Day a federal holiday.

The Tomb of the Unknowns is located in Arlington National Cemetery in Virginia.

Many people wrote to their representatives in Washington, D.C. to make Armistice Day a federal holiday.

Just like on Presidents' Day or Martin Luther King, Jr. Day, government offices were closed. There was no mail delivery. Schools, banks, and libraries were closed as well.

World War I had been called "the war to end all wars." People hoped there would never be another war. But, soon, different countries began fighting again. There were more wars.

That meant that there were other veterans, too. U.S. soldiers fought bravely in World War II and the Korean War. Many Americans thought there should be a holiday to honor all veterans, not just those who had fought in World War I. Once again, they asked their leaders to help. In 1954, President Dwight D. Eisenhower signed an important bill. November 11 became known as Veterans Day.

Later, Americans would fight in the Vietnam War and the Persian Gulf War. They often went to distant lands to keep the peace. Sometimes they died trying.

Veterans Day became a time to remember all those who served in the U.S. Armed Forces. People who died are remembered. So are the soldiers who came home. It does not matter which war they fought in. Veterans Day is for all veterans.

President Dwight D. Eisenhower signed an important bill in 1954 making November 11 Veterans Day.

Coast Guard Veterans Day memorial at Arlington National Cemetery, Virginia.

With the new holiday there were other changes, too. One was at the Tomb of the Unknowns. In 1958, two more soldiers were buried there. One had died in World War II. The other was killed in the Korean War. In 1984, a fourth soldier was also buried there. He died in the Vietnam War.

Each year on Veterans Day, a ceremony is held at the Tomb of the Unknowns. It always takes place on November 11 at exactly 11:00 A.M. The time and date are important. World War I stopped at 11:00 A.M. on November 11, 1918. That was the eleventh hour of the eleventh day of the eleventh month.

All the different military groups take part in the ceremony. There are two minutes of silence. No one speaks during that time, out of respect for the dead soldiers.

A wreath is placed at the tomb by the president of the United States. A military bugle song called "Taps" is played. Everyone stands quietly. It is a sad but important time. On Veterans Day, people remember those who died for America's freedom.

This ceremony is called The Changing of the Guard at the Tomb of the Unknowns.

CHAPTER 3

ACROSS AMERICA

Americans are proud of their veterans. They want these brave men and women to know how they feel. The ceremony at the Tomb of the Unknowns is important. But there are also many other ways to say thank you on Veterans Day.

Often these events are planned by veterans' groups. The members of these groups are veterans. They have joined together to work on different projects. Men and women who are still in the military usually help. They, too, are a part of Veterans Day ceremonies.

IN FLANDERS FIELDS

In World War I, a soldier named John McCrae wrote a poem called "In Flanders Fields." Poppies are still used to remember those who died on the battlefield. Part of it reads like this:

In Flanders Fields

In Flanders Fields
the poppies blow
Between the crosses,
row on row,
That mark our place;
and in the sky
The larks, still bravely
singing, fly
Scarce heard amid the
guns below.

We are the dead.
Short days ago
We lived, felt dawn,
saw sunset glow,
Loved and were loved,
and now we lie
In Flanders fields.

A memorial service is held
at this military cemetery.

Some ceremonies take place at soldiers' gravesites.
People across America gather at military cemeteries.
Often they are the families of veterans. Friends and
neighbors sometimes come, too. Veterans may also
attend these ceremonies. They can talk about what
happened to them in wartime.

Elected officials are usually there. They give speeches,
too. Flowers are placed on soldiers' graves.

Veterans are remembered in other ways, as well. In many places there are Veterans Day parades. Veterans' groups march in the parades. So do other people. High school marching bands play music. The songs show our pride in America.

There may be military vehicles in the parade also. Often there are floats, too. Many Veterans Day floats show patriotic scenes. They may be decorated with American flags. Some have red, white, and blue streamers.

Some Veterans Day parades have tanks in them.

23

Over 1,000 people march in New York City's Veterans Day parade. One veterans' group called Rolling Thunder takes part in the parade. Members of Rolling Thunder ride in the parade on shiny motorcycles.

Another group is the Rough Riders. They ride on horseback in the parade.

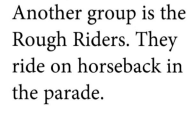

Veterans Day parades are always popular because people are proud of our nation's military and they want to show it!

Veterans Day parades are always popular. Everyone cheers for the marchers. People clap as the different veterans' groups pass. Some people wave small American flags. They are proud of our nation's military. They want to show it.

Some Veterans Day parades are large, like the one in New York City is. Other parades are small. This is not because people do not care or do not love their country. Sadly, as time passes, there are fewer veterans. Many have died. Others have become too old or too ill to march.

That was happening in Media, Pennsylvania. People there were worried about their Veterans Day parade. They wanted it to keep going in the future. But each year, fewer veterans marched.

Luckily, the mayor and some veterans' groups helped. They found a way to save the parade. They asked young people to march, too.

It is important to hold a parade every year on Veterans Day. We do not want to forget the people who fight to keep us free. This parade was held in Jackonsville, Florida.

Black POW-MIA flags remind us not to forget all the brave soldiers who were captured or were lost in battle.

"The emphasis really has to be on kids," Media's mayor Bob McMahon explained. "There is not going to be a parade in five or ten years if we do not involve kids now." Today, many young people march in Media's Veterans Day parade. Media also has a Flag Exchange ceremony at the parade. At this ceremony, the veterans give children special small flags. The flags are called POW-MIA flags.

POW stands for "Prisoner of War." These are soldiers who were taken prisoner by the enemy. MIA stands for "Missing in Action." These are soldiers who were lost in battle. No one knows what happened to them. They might have been taken prisoner or they might have been killed. Their bodies were never found.

POW-MIA flags are often seen at Veterans Day events. They remind us not to forget these brave soldiers. It is important to remember all our veterans.

Some people do this by wearing a special flower made of red paper on Veterans Day. The flowers are called poppies. The poppy is the official flower of a group called the Veterans of Foreign Wars (VFW). VFW members help us to remember other veterans.

The veterans give the poppies to people. In return, people give money to the veterans' group. The money is used to help veterans.

Poppy flowers are a reminder of the soldiers who died for our country.

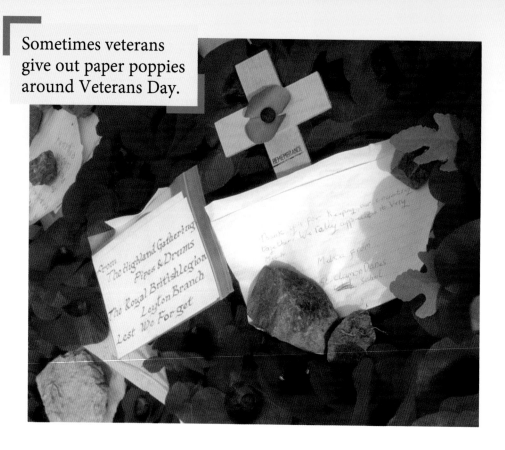

The poppy also has a special meaning. It was the subject of a famous poem called "In Flanders Fields." It was written by a soldier on the battlefield in World War I.

The soldier was a doctor who treated many dying men. Yet all around him poppies grew. That is because the flower only grows in rooted-up soil. The soil on battlefields is like that. Now poppies are a reminder of the soldiers who died.

Libraries often put out books about war on Veterans Day. There may also be books about military life.

Museums show weapons and military uniforms. Letters that soldiers sent home during wars are also shown.

Bakeries sell Veterans Day cakes and cupcakes. These have red, white, and blue frosting. Many places sell cookies in the shape of the American flag.

There are lots of real flags displayed on Veterans Day, too. Businesses may fly the American flag that day. Homeowners do the same.

For holidays such as Veterans Day, the Empire State Building is lit up in red, white and blue.

The Empire State Building is a very tall building in New York City. On Veterans Day, it is lit up in red, white, and blue. It can be seen for miles.

Veterans Day is a day for people all across the country to remember and thank veterans.

Master Sgt. Denise Williams looks on as Master Sgt. John Koehl makes a presentation about Veterans Day on Nov. 11 to a group of 4th and 5th graders at Alton Darby Creek Elementary School in Hilliard, Ohio.

CHAPTER 4

In Schools

Many schools put on special programs for Veterans Day. School bands may perform. They might play military marches. School choirs might sing patriotic songs like "America the Beautiful."

Sometimes veterans come to schools to speak to students. Young people learn what it is like to be a soldier, a fighter pilot, or a naval officer. Students also learn about being wounded. They find out how it feels to lose a friend in battle.

One Veterans Day program was extra special. It took place in Stamford, Connecticut. Twenty-two veterans came to Stamford High School. All had once been students at the

AMERICA THE BEAUTIFUL

One of the most patriotic songs we sing today is called "America the Beautiful." It was written in 1913 by Katharine Lee Bates to show her feelings about our country.

America the Beautiful

Oh beautiful, for
spacious skies,
For amber waves of grain,
For purple mountain
majesties
Above the fruited plain!
America! America!
God shed his grace on thee
And crown thy good with
brotherhood
From sea to shining sea!

Everyone was proud of the veterans who returned to school to receive their diplomas.

school nearly sixty years before. They had left before finishing school to fight in World War II. Now they were back to receive their high school diplomas.

It was a wonderful ceremony. Hundreds of students were there. Families, friends, and city officials came, too.

The audience stood up when the veterans came in. Students walked the men to the stage. Everyone clapped. Everyone was glad to be there. The high school principal said, "We must not miss this opportunity to say thank you." Everyone was proud of the veterans.

Not only veterans visit schools on Veterans Day. There may also be visits from servicemen and servicewomen who are in the military today. At one school, U.S. Marines came dressed in combat gear. Jeeps, cargo trucks, and tanks were also displayed. Students got a close-up view.

At times, schools have Veterans Day poster contests. Students make their own posters. Some draw soldiers or battle scenes. Their artwork shows what our veterans mean to us.

Art is often part of other Veterans Day school projects. Students in Fort Wayne, Indiana, remembered veterans through art. They made a wall of stars. First, they cut paper stars out of red, white, and blue paper. Then, they wrote the name of a different veteran on each star. The stars were put on the cafeteria wall. The students used the stars to make an American flag. Veterans who saw the wall were very proud.

We can show our appreciation for our veterans through cards or artwork.

For Verterans Day, some schools put on plays to show that the holiday is important to them.

In many schools, students write about Veterans Day. They write about why the holiday is important.

The best writing may be read at school programs. In some schools, the students' work is posted on bulletin boards so everyone can read it.

Schools' newspapers write about Veterans Day, too. Student reporters may speak to veterans. The veterans might be family members or people in the community. The reporters write about the veterans' experiences. These make very interesting stories.

In some towns, red, white, and blue balloons are released as part of a Veterans Day celebration.

In 2002, soldiers were sent to Afghanistan during Operation Enduring Freedom. Children in the United States sent them letters and cards to let the soldiers know that they appreciated all they did to keep Americans safe.

Veterans Day is a day to remember and thank our veterans. Often, students find ways to do this. They may make thank-you cards. On the outside they might draw a soldier or a flag. Inside, they write a thank-you message. Their teacher takes the cards to a veterans' hospital.

Veterans like getting these special cards on their holiday. The cards show the veterans that people have not forgotten that they fought for the freedom of America.

Soldiers and veterans are always grateful to receive letters from people.

ear soldiesrs,
hope your having a grate time.
'll Pray for you. you.
od bless you.

your Friend claire

North Pontotoc Ele
Pontotoc, MS
october 6, 2004

Dear soldier,

My name is Holly
I'm eight years old. I'm going
to ask you some questions.
Are you coming home for Thanksgiving
Do you have a family?
Is this your first time
in the war? Now I'm going
to tell you about some stuff.
My new cousin's sister is in
the war her name is Robin.
Your really missing the fall
leaves. Every body is picking
out halloween costums and
picking out pumkins. What
branch of the war are you
in? Your being so brave
to go out and fight for
our freedom! Do you ever
get nerves in the night
that some one is going to
sneak up on you?

Your Friend
Holly

The U.S. Post Office saluted women in the military with a special stamp. Former Air Force Captain Lillian Kinkela holds a drawing of the "Women in Military Service" stamp. Kinkela is the highest-decorated woman in the history of the U.S. Military.

LOOKING AHEAD

From 1900 to 1999, veterans were often called upon to fight. Each time, they came to our nation's defense. The year 2000 brought still new ways to remember these brave men and women.

The U.S. Postal Service put out three new stamps for Veterans Day. All the new stamps honored World War II veterans.

Veterans Day 2000 was important for another reason. Work on the World War II Memorial in Washington, D.C., began then. A memorial is a monument or statue that is a reminder of a person or event. This memorial honors World War II veterans. There are over 16 million veterans from World War II.

THE AMERICAN BALD EAGLE

On June 20, 1782, the bald eagle was chosen as the emblem of the United States. The eagle represents freedom. It was chosen because of its majestic look, long life, and great strength.

There are many war memorials, like this one commemorating the raising of the flag after fierce fighting on Iwo Jima in World War II.

President Bill Clinton dug the first few shovelsful of earth to start the building. Military bands played. There were large television screens at the site. They showed scenes from World War II.

Many people had looked forward to that day. They had worked hard for it. For thirteen years, they had raised money for the memorial.

One of those people was a man named Tom Schepers. He is a Vietnam veteran who was hurt while fighting. No one expected him to walk again. But he did walk. Later, he was even able to run.

Veterans Day is an important day for all Americans.

Sometimes, Schepers ran to help veterans. He would run for miles. Newspapers and magazines wrote about him. He told them why he ran. It helped to make the needs of veterans known.

In 2000, Tom Schepers went on a special run to honor World World II veterans. The run began on June 6. Schepers started out from Camp Pendleton, a marine training base in California. The run ended on Veterans Day at the World War II Memorial in Washington, D.C. He had run over 3,300 miles!

Veterans Day is an important time for veterans. But it is also a special day for all Americans. It is a day to honor those who protect us.

Veterans Day Craft

Veterans Day Thank-you Card

Make a thank-you card and give it to a veteran on Veterans Day. You might give it to a member of your family who is a veteran. You can also give it to someone else. Any veteran will be glad to know you care. You will need:

★ **A piece of blue construction paper**
★ **Red and silver stick-on stars**
★ **A black magic marker**
★ **A stack of old magazines**
★ **Safety scissors**
★ **White glue**

1. Fold the piece of blue paper in half from one short end to the other. This is your card.

2. Decorate the outside of the card with the stick-on stars.

3. Use the black magic marker to write the words "THANK YOU" on the front of the card.

4. Think about why you are grateful to our veterans. Then look through the magazines. Find the picture that best shows your feelings.

5. Cut the picture out and glue it inside your card.

6. Write your own message next to the picture.

*Safety Note: Be sure to ask for help from an adult, if needed, to complete this project.

Veterans Day Craft

Let's get started!

You can think of other ways to decorate your card, too!

Thank you for keeping me safe! Thank you for watching over the Country!

Alison

Thank-you cards ready to be given to a veteran!

Dear Veterans,
Thank you so much for all you do for our country! And thank you for helping to make the USA the Land of the Free!

-Thank you
Kara

Write your message inside.

Words to Know

armistice—An agreement to stop fighting.

bill—A plan for a new law.

century—One hundred years.

democracy—A government that is run by the people who live under its rules.

emblem—A symbol that stands for an idea.

memorial—A reminder of a person or an event.

mosque—A Muslim place to pray.

patriotic—Showing love for one's country.

truce—An agreement by enemies to stop fighting.

veteran—A person who has served in the armed forces.

Read More About

Brill, Marlene Targ. *Veterans Day*. Minneapolis, MN:
Carolrhoda Books, 2005.

Catalanotto, Peter. *The Veterans Day Visitor*. New York, NY:
Henry Holt and Company, LLC., 2008.

Nelson, Robin. *Veterans Day*. Minneapolis, MN: Lerner
Publications Company, 2006.

Internet Addresses

VA KIDS, K-5TH
  <http://www.va.gov/kids/k-5/index.asp>
  *A web site dedicated to educating kids about veterans
  including games and activities and links.*

APPLES4THETEACHER
  **<http://www.apples4theteacher.com/holidays/veterans-day/
  when-is-veterans-day.html>**
  This is a fun educational web site for teachers and kids.

KABOOSE
  <http://www.kaboose.com/search.html?q=veterans+day>
  *This web site includes activities, crafts and printables
  for children.*

Index